Poetic Dawn

An Anthology of Poetry

Edited By Amanda Read

δ

Published by Dogma Publications

Dogma Publications 3 Fulmar Lane Wellingborough
Northants NN8 4AE England

Poetic Dawn

Cover picture taken from François Boucher's
The Rising of the Sun
1753
Wallace Collection, London

First Published 2004
by Dogma Publications

ISBN 1-84591-003-6

Printed in Great Britain for Dogma Publications

Poetic Dawn

Contents

Contents Continued

Contents Continued

Winter Poem In Praise Of Rosy's Knitting

Everyday I wear garments knitted by you.
That I have so many is a testament to your craft and generosity;
Cardigans for work, sweaters for the weekend and
A long evening jacket sumptuous in Royal Blue.
The patterns are intricate and various, Arrans and Fair Isle,
The colours bold and subtle.
Some are feather soft and light,
others as heavy as a sheep's coat and as snug.
They provide my Winter warmth and cover my heart.
Hours of your life are held in perfect stitch and twist of yarn.
I think of you whenever I wear them.
Everyday I wear garments knitted by you.

Elizabeth Sandeman

Splinter In My Heart

You attacked hard
Left a constant pain
Not at all the same
Since you flew away
It's hard to say
It's like you threw a wooden dart
And it left a tiny splinter deep within my heart.

Sitting on a Friday night
Reading under the light
Finding it hard to believe
You were ever going to leave
It's like you threw a wooden dart
And it left a tiny splinter deep within my heart.

Looking through the picture book
Before my heart you took
Tears splattered on the page
Trapping me inside a cage
It's like you threw a wooden dart
And it left a tiny splinter deep within my heart.

Wrapped up nice and warm
Getting close to the break of dawn
Just trying to forgive
I just need to live
I'm not a kid
So I can forgive you for what you did
It's like you threw a wooden dart
And it left a tiny splinter deep within my heart.

Lucy Green

September 13th

A seeping rupture from my bite,
The wicked storyteller of that vicious night,
When in one blurry, sorry hour,
The bond between two brothers crumbled,
As vintage seized its power.

'From this first punch all fun will end
And love and joy will neither fix nor mend.
You will spill blood and I tears,
And from this day forward I'll never forget
The pounding in my ears.'

If I could've stopped the shards of glass,
Frozen them in mid air,
I'd have said, 'Lets end this silly farce',
And through the crystal, knife-like rain I'd walk,
My body bruised and bare.

Matthew Pinkett

Suzanne's Sonnet

Don't smile as you tell me you love me.
Don't smile as you tell me your lies.
I can tell by your look,
(Like an often read book),
The truth that you try to disguise.
And I doubt you'll remember me fondly.
Doubt you'll even remember my name.
Just a notch on your bed,
Once the passion has fled.
Yes, I think I remember this game.

Steven Waterfield

He Slipped Away

He slipped away like morning dew
Before the sun was high.
Back to his den by the railway track,
To dream of days gone by.

To days when the town were fields of green.
When people and cars were rarely seen.
When fox cubs played in the cool night air,
Could run for miles, go anywhere.

Now the green has turned to grey.
Man took his countryside away.
The natural woodlands, where once they ran
Is now a concrete jungle made by man.

Linda Ludlow

Just A Dream

You whisper softly in my ear,
How sweet the sound;
You say those words I long to hear
I'm spinning round.
You run your fingers through
My hair,
My hands reach out, but you're
Not there.

Cold light of day
You've slipped away
Ah! - Just a dream.

Your fingers touch my fingertips,
tenderly,
Now your lips are on my lips,
You're kissing me.
Your arms are open wide,
Now enfolding me inside.
Please don't let go,
I've missed you so.

Breaks the dawn
Again you're gone
Ah! - Just a dream.

Faith Spencer

Safely Home

I am home in HEAVEN dear ones
Oh! So happy and so bright
There is perfect joy and beauty
In this everlasting light
All the pain and grief is over
Every restless tossing past
I am now at peace forever
SAFELY HOME, in HEAVEN at last
Did you wonder, I so calmly
Trod the valley of the shade
Oh! But JESUES love illumined
Every dark and fearful glade
And HE came, Himself to meet me
In that way so hard to tread
And with JESUES' arm to lean on
Could I have one doubt or dread
Then you must not grieve so sorely
For I love you dearly still
Try to look beyond earth's shadows
Pray to trust our FATHER'S will
There is work still waiting for you
So you must not idly stand
Do it now while life remaineth
You shall rest in JESUS land
When that work is all completed
HE will gently call you home
Oh! The rapture of the meeting
Oh! The joy to see you come.

A S Price

Dancing In The Park

Mussolini struts, holding court,
Ranting into his mobile phone,
Stamping, waving arms,
Pouting, posing, pelvic thrusting.
Shame it isn't even turned on.

Acid party in the park.
L S D-isembodied imperatives pulse
From over large speakers.
Big Issue sellers, on their day off,
Dance staccato,
Their dogs look on bewildered,
And mill around.
Skinny hipped students from nice homes
Pretend to belong,
Mummy's car discreetly parked out of view.
Roll up culture hard at play.
It's cheaper than a pint of beer,
So come into my office,
And buy, from the boot of my car.
Dance yourself silly,
Oops, I see, you already are..

Darren does stunning tricks with his football,
Admiring girls look on, some impressed.
He will brag to his mates how he scored today.

Pill pushers shiftily sort their wares
From out of the back of the car,
Into their deep combat pockets.

Fat man, huge overhang belly,
Does the crossword, blissfully unaware,
As the Emergency Ambulance
Slowly arrives on the scene...

Bill Read

Forever Free

So - how much do I love you? In what ways?
what red-dipped sunset and what burning dawn
can drain this cup of loving or amaze
me more than you, who, earthbound, bold, still yawns
at poems of love, stretching the long-ribbed spine
of sinuous life with a cat-like ease,
content to be yourself, not ever mine
nor his, nor anyone's: forever free.
So - measurements of loving tap a stream
that feels fathomless to man, while woman
weeps to fashion the mysteries we dream
knowing the deep pool quiescent I am;
hence, how much, here, I rhythm out above:
the rest is, silently, an endless love.

Jill Jameson

Soul Hues

Be still my heart, yet run to depths of glory
There is solace in the sky, with hints of
passion adorning
Askance the dawning with a night owl
clawing and yawning.

Love scatter its petals across the morn
to murmur and catch the sweet dew with
lips aching and moaning for flesh to
suckle and gasp with lascivious yearning
The morning has woken, and all is golden.

Doran St George

The Promise

When you breakdown
I will lift you up
When you slip and fall
I will catch you
When you go astray
I will guide you
When you fall in love
I will be your friend
When you lose your mind
I will restore your soul
When you fall out of love
I will let you go
When you are all at sea
I will be your lighthouse
When death's angel makes you shiver
I will kiss you still.

Alexander Prosper

Arbre Vitae

We owe a great debt to trees
They were houses, boats, fuel for us;
They harboured the holy in their sacred groves.
Without trees as wood or in fossilised form
No warmth would have comforted us
At night or in winter's drear days,
No cooking pot would have spread
The appetizing odours of simmering food,
No interwoven branches would have sheltered us.

Now, too clever by half, as the saying is,
We spin our warmth from electrons
Or trap the rays of old Sol
In batteries of low-impact technology.
We make our ships from shining cold steel,
Our homes we mass-make from relentless cement.

Cut down are the sacred groves for motorways;
The holy has retreated, obsolescent
For all but a few, who, in their hearts
Keep alive the need and the search for that
Which could fill the void at the heart of our being.

Margaret Chisman

Autumn In Hanningfield

I went abroad without you today,
Passed woodside and lake and bare fields on my way.
The fields lay bereft of their gold summer crop.
The trees, not quite leafless, just thinning on top -
Their pride turned to copper and sailed to the ground,
The wind quite too lazy to push them around.
The lake was a mirror this calm autumn day:-
There's no public access. There's no right of way.

I went abroad without you today,
The sun kept on shining, the clouds stayed away.
The old church, well buttressed. The steeple still proud
Guards homesteads and forebears, the landscape about
So tidy, so lonely, so still and so locked -
The people are missing, the bell-summoned flock.
No prayers to rise in a tallow light's glow,
No song lifting spirits, no friends said hello.

I went abroad without you today,
The woods brooding sombre, no pleasure to stay.
The kestrel still hover'd, the sky was still blue,
But the first not as high and the latter not true.
The oak tried its best, the maple encore -
Their last glow of colour now cushions the floor.
But brambles are plenty, crab apples and sloes
In thickets of darkness. No sign of a rose.

I went abroad without you today.
Boot scrapers un-scraped, melancholia held sway.

Robert Hallmann

Down Memory Lane

As I dander down the back lane,
My heart is full of glee,
I climbed the gate in front of me,
Too lazy to open it properly.

My mind is full of wonder,
As I stride along,
The birds are singing cheerfully,
As the rabbits hop along.

The wild roses are growing vigorously,
I carefully pick out a branch,
The smell it is divine,
Mine you! I let it go again,
As the bugs I didn't like.

The cows are grazing contently,
Their morning's work all done,
The river bed is flowing,
A soft and gentle run.

I sat down to have a rest,
The distance I'd gone is far,
The beauty of the countryside,
Fills my heart with joy.

In the distance I hear my name,
I scrambled to my feet and ran to the gate,
When I reached the back door,
My Mum she said, 'Where have you been?'

I smiled a cheeky grin as I replied,
'Down by the river Ma!'
'Oh I see!'

‘The tea is ready, wash your hands!’
I hope your feet are clean!’
I removed my wellies as I went in.
Oh what fond memories I have of my wee Mum.

Carole Herron

Despair So Colourful

This desert, just deserted, the sand tells my story,
This ocean, just beauty, the waves read my mind,
This sky, captures life, the clouds bring me hope,
This landscape, it means freedom, the emptiness clears my head.

Repetition, they said holds down all deceit,
The words, I was told would break all my bones,
This music, I was asked, was it nightmares in words?
And my nightmares, they predicted, would project all insanity.

The blood, that was cried, was a treat in itself,
The cold, which numbed me, slowly made my day,
The despair, with sweet tastes, rebuilt my creation,
The love, that I shared, only postponed a filthy ending.

The white, overpowering purity, it staged my mind,
The red, inside me, I used as integrity and to sleep at night,
The blue, I marvelled, as I sat and wondered about evenings,
The black, helped destroy me; I'm confused in this darkness.

The insults, were a simple excuse, to dream of better days,
The finality, wouldn't crush me, only my beliefs,
The changes, my problem, left me petrified,
Your anger, colourful, leaves me thoughtful; awaiting the end.

Sophie Daysh

Across A Room

And in a flash
I saw and knew you
Across the room
Your eyes met mine
And in that glance
Your smile enhanced me
And I just knew this was our time.

You were alone and looking radiant
I looked away and you were there
Now close beside me
So pale, so fair.

You must have known that all I wanted
In all the world was only you.

Why had we waited
Were we too shy
To say 'I need you'
Was not a lie.

And from that moment we both decided
That as one we'd face the world
And so forever we'll both go forward
As hand in hand we take what comes.

We'll share the best times and the bad times
We'll take whatever comes our way.

But it's ok as long as I have you.

And in a flash
I saw and knew you
Across the room
Your eyes met mine.

Julie Hepworth

Crimson

Rolling across fields
Our childish giggles
Pollen dancing in the air
Our smiling faces.

Running after you
Along the wet sand
The waves
Roaring.

Walking down the road
Rain soaked hair
Clinging to my back
Alone.

Crying at my window
The gray sky
Wind rattling the pane of glass
Tears rolling down my cheeks.

Shining dagger in my hand
Crimson puddle
Cold tugging at my fingers.

I'll be with you soon.

Samantha Morgan

A Little Comic Relief (Or Not)

The taxman, the taxman
A devil in disguise.
He says we owe him lots more dosh.
Not true we say, all lies!

We both work hard all through the year
To keep our house so nice.
And now he says, not good enough
And wants a bigger slice.

It's B&B for seven months.
That means we cook and clean.
But in the Winter when we're shut
There's other tasks unseen.

There's all the linen to be washed
And one must man the phone.
The painting, papering and repairs
Means one must stay at home.

Some carpets need a big shampoo.
There's furniture to shift.
New pictures hung, the windows cleaned
To give the house a lift.

With no one in, we have the chance
To clean each nook and cranny.
The shower drains and ceiling fans
It all must be quite sani.

We try our best, work never stops.
A clean house is a must.
This persecution isn't right.
It fact it's most unjust.

Kathryn Spence

Merton Priory

Many a season has come and gone,
Since these old walls heard such fine song,
In Merton, home to King and Pope
The cradle of this nation's hope
Of all we were, and still might be,
If those in power could only see...
Could only see and but embrace
The sanctity of this holy place,
Where Becket and Breakspear walked in prayer.
Breathed the sweet savour of Merton's air
And grace and peace held quiet sway
Following St. Augustine's way.

Christine Stokes

It's Always On A Sunday

On a cold wet Sunday morning,
when everyone else is fast asleep.
There are some folk that get up early,
To muck out and give yards a sweep.
Yes us folk that work in racing,
We work all hours of the day.
With one full day off every fortnight,
and we get very little pay.
How is it when you've just got finished,
got swept up and made yourself a brew.
You get that unexpected visit,
from your owner in his BMW.
So you go out and get the horse ready,
make it look nice and put it on show.
How these people have such good timing,
is something I never will know.
But just to see the horse, isn't quite good enough,
you have to tack up and ride the horse out.
And how is it when your owners there watching,
your horse is fresh and starts pratting about.
So you take him home, and put him in stable,
your polite and give a big smile.
Is this nice man gonna pull out a tenna,
to make your Sunday all the more worthwhile.
If the answers no, then I truly am sorry,
but in most cases, this is very true.
All we ask is a little bit of gratitude,
for all the hard work that we do.
Yes us folk that work in racing,
we are grafters, and are a rare breed.
For without us the whole racing industry,
would never ever succeed!

Sarah Perry

Mirror

Honesty that cannot lie
Is what in a mirror you would spy
Whatever before it stands
An exact copy to you a mirror hands.

A mirror shows only what it sees
And it does so with reflective ease
Flat mirroring glass it bears
No emotion, feelings, or mortal cares.

So do not look into mirror
If what you seek is lies
For to you it will show a shocking surprise
Truth is what the mirror does hold
To you, for no price, is what it has sold.

If reality is what you detest
A mirror to you is but a failed test
If things real is what you seek
Then, maybe, just maybe
You should take a peek.

Danny Pegg

Queen Mary's 'F' Ward

They put me in the 'Old Ladies' ward
My God; what a shock to the system
A mistake of course-from the very start
But never mind-I'll play the part-
I'll put my teeth in a plastic bowl
I'll listen to Wagner instead of Soul
I'll show all the 'Crepey' bits of my skin
And wish to God I'd never come in.

G Barton

Extinguished Life?

Today's pain or tomorrow's heartache
My choice as I lie in my bed alone. Unrest and feelings
of wretched helplessness my only comfort.

My head a weight. My eyes blinded by drops of falling pearls
that wet the blankets that warm me where your arms
should have lain.

I scream my despair, yet no one hears.
Wrapped in isolation my life's objectives, you, have left me.
My heart breaks in my despair, yet no one can pick up the pieces.
It is in isolation, it's subject, you, have left me.
My stomach churns with despair, despair being my only protein,
since you, my food of life, have left me.

The night engulfs my room and the rain stabs
against the windows. My room as dark as the night
proves a mere shadow compared to the bleakness within me.

Yet, I know this rigid, zombie-like stance cannot be maintained.

Joanne Armstrong

Isn't It Amazing?

Isn't it amazing?
What we see, hear and do,
For we have seen wonders,
And we have heard the good news
And we have done our fathers will,
Go little children to all nations,
Telling them Jesus is his name.

Isn't it amazing?
That the word became flesh,
He was borne of Mary,
The virgin mother, Jesus was his name,
He would be the Saviour of the world,
To take the sin away.

Isn't it amazing?
What He can do,
As we look around in the world today,
So many lives being changed,
Drug addictions to praising God,
Jesus can change you,
And make you a different person.

Isn't it so good?
Jesus was born to save us,
From this evil world,
And to do his Fathers will,
He was born to be holy,
Born to give us a chance,
To know and understand.

Kathy Stewart

The Rain

A billion drops of rain
Lie resting in placid pools
Doubling the landscape
And giving the sky a twin.
Their newly found unison
Responding only to gravity
And the mortifying wind
Fresh from the Gulags.

Vapourised by the sun
The pools rise mistily
And vanish slowly
Writhing in pain from
The slow transformation
According to laws written
In the distant genesis
Of the Big Bang.

Mike O'Brien

Which Path Should I Choose?

There are paths to be chosen,
Choices to be made.
But which ones are the right ones?
Into deeper waters, I wade.

On the crossroads here I stand, looking for a sign or an arrow.
But which path will be chosen, wide, short, long or narrow?
Many problems will arise,
On all the paths open to choose.
They bend and they twist,
Each way I can loose.

But which path will be chosen?
And will it be today?
How long will I stand and ponder,
And keep wondering 'which way?'

There are steps to be taken,
Choices to be made
But on the table of destiny,
There, my cards are laid.

Siân Bevins

My Love

When I look at you I see a Summer's morn,
One that has never been torn.
When I saw those eyes looking at me,
I knew you were the man for me.
Standing there with so much grace,
And you had a gorgeous face.
When I think of you I think of love,
Accompanied by a flying dove.
While with you I'll do my best
I'd even climb Mount Everest.
When with you I have no need for tears,
You even banish all my fears.
When I gaze at your face I see a mid Summer's dream,
One that contains a pretty little stream.
My love for you will always be burning,
And my heart will always be yearning.
I want to spend my whole life with you,
And I hope you feel the same way too.

Vicki Gaffney

Nothingness

Nothingness is boring and uncreated,
No one to talk to, it's isolated.
It is dark, old, and godforsaken,
You think to yourself you'll never awaken.

It's so silent and so still,
Oh no, I haven't wrote a will.
Cold and wet this stupid weather,
Will I be here forever and ever?

It's so empty and so lonely too,
I want to see my family if only I could do.
I think I'm dead I do not know,
Will I soon see a bright torch glow?

Probably not, I could be forgotten,
But I hate this place it feels so rotten.
I'll just have to get used to it if I'm going to live here now,
Maybe I'll come back into the world someday, somehow.

I wonder how it happened am I stuck here forever,
Maybe I was killed by a man called Trevor.
Or was there something wrong, a disease or a thing like that,
Maybe it was an animal, a dirty little rat.

Or it could be Shiva from the Hindu creation story,
Maybe I am Brahma, that couldn't be me surely.
Is the world dead too, are they suffering this hell,
A dark, cold, lonely world just like an everlasting well.

These people cannot live like this I must try to stop it,
Is this possible or are we stuck in this cold and dark closet?
Forever In Nothingness,
In Nothingness Forever!

Kathryn Brown

Feminine Side

I'm in touch with my feminine side
I can tolerate quiche
And I've even tried
To avert my gaze
When bosoms collide
I'm in touch with my feminine side.

I'm not a sexist per se
I iron, I Hoover
Put dishes away
Don't need to make conquests
To prove I'm not gay
I'm not a sexist per se.

I'm a sensitive man with the facts
About all things "Gynie"
About tubes and tracts
I don't get embarrassed
Buying a box of Tampax
I'm a sensitive man with the facts.

I'm gentle and loving in bed
I know where the clit is
And like giving head
You don't have to swallow
Just cuddle instead
I'm gentle and loving in bed.

I'm in touch with my feminine side
It'll come as no shock
To find out I lied
Just five minutes after
I've slipped one inside
I may be in touch
But we don't coincide.

In fact can't remember the last time we spoke
I only said it as a bit of a joke
To persuade you into
A prod and a poke
Let's face it love
I'm a bloke.

Chris Morris

Heaven's Above

When I'm asleep I dream the angels
take me by the hand.
And lead me to another place,
a far off distant land.
Where all around there's happiness,
and little birds all sing.
Amidst the warmth of sunshine,
and every day is Spring.
But we are not in Heaven yet,
so let us share a smile.
And help each other every day,
by making life worthwhile!

Ann Wilson

A Sudden Loss

Where have you gone to? You're not here anymore.
Did you know you were leaving
When you walked out the door?

Did you bother with packing your toothbrush and comb?
Did you know you were leaving
And not coming home?

There's an empty space. An aching hollow.
Did you know you were leaving
And no-one to follow?

We'll feel better in time. We'll heal in a while.
Did you know you were leaving
And taking your smile?

Did you know that we loved you? You knew that we might.
Did you know you were leaving?
Did you put up a fight?

We'll think of you often, with a tear and a sigh.
We didn't know you were leaving.
We didn't say goodbye.

Marilyn Prowse

Love Haiku

My tea tastes different
When it is made by you, dear
It tastes of your love.

Hazel Buckingham

A Million Dreams

I've had a million dreams about you
And all the things we could do
We could catch a movie, or just sit and talk
Holding hands while we walk
I could tell you what I've kept inside
All the things I tried to hide
Only in dreams can I tell you what's true
Cause you'd break my heart and tear it in two

Sometimes I dream you take me away
Everything's so perfect, I want you to stay
Sometimes I dream of us by the sea
Holding me close, where I'm meant to be
Heart's about to burst, beating so fast
Consumed by these feelings, wanting to last

This dream I know I'll never forget
Gentle whispers, watching sunset
Your eyes spoke words I'd wanted to hear
But soon my dream will disappear
And I'll have to wake knowing nothing is real
Just something made up, wounds that will never heal
You will never feel the same, there's nothing I can do
Because I've had a million dreams about you

And not one has come true...

Zoe Eggleton

What Are

What are promises but spoken words
Empty hollows, covers truth.
What is love that only wounds
Deceitful lies, without proof.

What is my heart but flesh and blood
Beating hard but broken.
What are these eyes that cause the flood
Painful tears, a novel token.

What is my mind but a store of knowledge
Times I've cried, times I've smiled.
What is my future but lack of courage
Scared of truth, eternal trial.

What is my life but an endless night
Cold that burns, dark that smothers.
What is my soul but what doesn't matter
Spiritual essence, my only savour.

What is loneliness, this I feel inside
Absence of love, a child's nightmare.
What is innocence but unaware
Harsh reality, no one cares.

I see no hope for me with my denunciation.
I tried so hard to please you, my desperation.
Take me for who I am but not for granted.
When I have left you, you'll feel my sting implanted.

You have made me all hating.
Longing in the dark
I'm still waiting.

Donna Kent

Falling Apart

He'd obsess with couple's bliss
the heartache and the way she kissed
She always thought 'there's more than this'
She held his hand, he held her fist
He's falling apart
When she breaks his heart.

He's insecure and likes to swing
to fall in love, and then to cling
In his mind, he is her king
His makeup is her favourite thing,
He's falling apart
When she breaks his heart.

Rebecca Wass

Mirror

Love's dream is to be reflected,
To see a perfect image of itself staring back,
Unblinking,
Unmoving.
I know of this,
As I know of the aching stare,
When the reflections ripple,
When love feels like a vampire,
Looking, but seeing nothing there.

Andrea Gillman

Turbulence

What is this darkness dwelling in my blood
That hath no purpose? Wherefore do I quake
And rage in equal measure? Whence this flood
Of bitter meditations? For the sake
Of sanity, must I near go insane:
Intoxication, sweet yet bitt'r as gall,
Through liquor, lust and drugs, though most profane,
Brings tainted bliss, e'en as it doth appall!
And what of sacred joys? My will is not
To gaze most righteous from a lofty height
With scorn, nor, having worldly strife forgot,
To bask in holy transports of delight.
Do I blaspheme? Aye, truly; but be sure:
I've borne this much, but cannot bear much more.

James Farrell

Colour Blind

And so I've lived
For one more day
In the rainbow land
Where I'm colour blind.

Choked on a lie
Bound by a tale
Embroidered the truth
Let reality pale.

And so I've lived
For one more day
In the rainbow land
Where I'm colour blind.

Crumbling heart
Stumbling and worn
Charred black and burning
Finally torn.

And so I've lived
For one more day
In the rainbow land
Where I'm colour blind.

Shattering soul
Smoke-like and pale
Glass-like it's breaking
Cracking and frail.

And so I lived
For one last day
In the rainbow land
Where I'm colour blind.

Lying, dying
Hide in a wail
To fall to the floor
And finally fail.

Hannah Sayers

The Luddite's Ode

A pencil weaves its winding way,
  planned or not, between the lines.
The hand that holds, the poise controlled;
  a poet writes, but thinks of rhymes.

What joy it is to write so well
  without a thought of one's technique
Of putting marks down: uprights, arcs
  that do the heart's own language speak!

The mundane and the practical
  the pigeonholed belief endorse
But see not this, and that do miss
  which plainly does not prompt discourse.

So now their word-processor's come
  and banished all our pens and ink,
The pencil with its humble fill,
  in favour of machines that "think".

For now one needs to concentrate
  (and poets' words are dangerous)
Not on rhyme, for that's sublime
  but miskeying's ridiculous!

Simon North-Keeling

Encompassed By The Beauty Of The Dying Sun

Golden translucence covers the sky like a blanket,
Saying farewell to the day, as azure atmosphere fades away;
Strands of brilliance blend into shades of pure midnight,
Forming tarnished needles of dusk sewn into the sky;
The coming night appears suffocating and heavy,
Unfamiliar mourning as sunlight fades to night,
Blurring the world as velvet layers close in over me,
Fused together with the day to form natures delight.

Eyes, declaring themselves witnesses to days final breath,
Create natural prisms of sunlight and emotion...
...ardent pleas for the perfection to never end;
Slowly the tears begin to overflow...
...crystal drops of anguish creating ripples through the aging air.
As my heart tries to match the beauty in the heavens,
For this magnificent spectacle,
opposing the darkness in my own heart,
Opens up new windows, lets the emotions fly free,
And I feel so alone...encompassed by the beauty of the dying sun...

Phyllis Thompson

Call Yourself A Mother

You had a loving husband
and a daughter who cared as well.
But your cold and selfish attitude
made our lives a living Hell.

There were no hugs and kisses
and no 'Well Done's' were said.
Just a look that was vile
that filled me with dread.

As an adult I left home to start up on my own
even then your attitude would not leave me alone.
My visits were frequent
Your silence long
I'd go home and cry
I couldn't be strong.

When my dad lay dying in his hospital bed
You got rid of his clothes, he was not even dead.

You were no mother
You were no wife
We were unlucky to get you
in the lottery of life.

Lynne Owen

Granny

You were so special all our lives,
Your parting leaves us grieving.
On special times we think of you
And the joy you brought to our hearts
Is there once more.
GRANNY
This is the name you liked to be used.
'I'm not your Nanny, I'm your Granny'
You would say and so even today it brings a smile
When we hear this word.
GRANNY
You have gone to be with Granddad,
Which if we're honest we know is where you should be
And we find comfort knowing he's there
GRANNY
Rest well now for you worked hard for 89 years
And now your love lives on in us.
You will be treasured in our hearts forever
And never be forgotten.

Lorraine Cleggett

Mixed Emotions

It makes me feel numb,
It makes me ashamed,
It makes me calm down,
It makes me feel safe.

How can one thing
Provoke such varied emotions?
One dangerous thing
Causes so much commotion

Once it starts,
It's with you forever,
No matter how much
You try to get better

You get back on your feet;
One step at a time,
And pray for escapism,
From the day and the night

Inside you know it can never be,
You have to deal with it,
Just like me.

Dawn Genner

Brighton Beach On A Summer Morn

The smell of the sea, as it wafts in the breeze so free.
The salty aroma from the coast far yonder,
one of natures gifts I wonder.

On a early summer-morn, just before break of dawn.
No pollution in the air, the beaches are barren and bare.
No flesh a roasting, basting its self in Ambre Solaire.

The beach-comber is out on the virgin sand,
his metal-detector and trowel in hand.
Waiting to hear the bleep from the sand, is it a gold coin or a pull-top
from an old drink can.

There is a couple a walking hand-in-hand, barefooted in the sand.
Scrawling, their love for each other in the sand, and watching it gently
get slowly washed away, and hoping their love last many a-day.
All on a summer-morn, just before the break of dawn.

Paul-John Harris

How Honest Is Honest?

I want to be honest
I want to be thought of as an honest person
honestly honest as I know what it is to be honest
so that I can be as honest as I know how much of honesty is honest.

I want to be honest so that I am loved for being honest
but when I am rejected for being hurtfully honest
then I am not loved for being honest but rejected for being hurtful
so I am afraid to be honest lest I hurt and be rejected
and being rejected I cannot honestly be any more loving
that I can be honestly loved.

If I make you angry I am not loved
If I am honest I may make you angry
If I am honest you are angry
and best of all if I am not honest I am angry with myself for making
you angry whether I am honest or not.

I feel guilty for being angry for having been honest
I am angry for feeling guilty for having been angry
I am guilty of making you angry by being honest
I must not be honest in case I feel upset by you being angry with me
for feeling guilty for having been angry with you
for being angry with me for having been honest with you…

Perhaps I don't want to be honest but I want to be hurtful?
Under the cloak of public honesty a little private cruelty?
A little private power, a spoonful of whitewash,
a dash of manufactured reason,
a square of honest anger, a tumble of sympathy
and I can be loved for my private parts
and admired for my public honesty
while I exercise my secret cruelty
and am respected for being both powerful and honest
while I pretend to be listening attentively
but really feel evasive and withdrawn.

After all I may fall in love with you
and you might laugh at me and I might be hurt.
so I torture myself and turn my cruelty against myself
and indulge myself in self pity
for being honest and dishonest and cruel
and hurtful and uncompromising and poor me.

Hans Lobstein

For Those Who Think

For those who think that heaven
Is there for when you die
Just taste the bread unleaven
In a church that stands near by.

You'll find that it's around you
Here and every day
You only have to hear the sound
Of children as they play.

My little bit of heaven
Is here on earth for me
A car trip down to Devon
My Granddaughter to see.

For some it may be fishing
A time to contemplate
So what if they are wishing
For a fish to fill their plate.

Its in the peace and solitude
You feel that God is near
No need to eat your full of food
God will fill you He is near.

To watch the waves come in a roll
As far as the eye can see
Such awe and wonder fill the soul
God is so very near to me.

Sheila King

Seasons

Winter grey skies
Snowflakes falling, crisp and white
Ponds frozen, skaters' delight.
Spring, rebirth.
Crocus, snowdrops, buds on trees
Calves, lambs staying close to mum.
Summer sunshine skies of blue
Time in the park, days on the beach.
Paddling, ice cream.
Picnics to eat.
Autumn, wind and rain.
Leaves turn crisp, brown and gold
The end of a year
Begins to unfold.

Pam Twiselton

An Ancient Land

As my poem unfolds,
of the days of old.
In ancient Egypt where
pyramids stand bold,
There are Kings and Queens,
Dressed in there splendour,
Princes and Princesses,
Small and Slender,
With their riches
and their jewels.

They were very clever,
The way they ruled,
So when the end was near,
There was no fear,
They were embalmed and buried,
With things they held dear.

Lilian Pass

Did I Ever Tell You?

Did I ever tell you
What you really mean to me?
You crept into my heart
Like we were meant to be
Did I ever tell you
Your smile lit up my day?
You were always there to cheer me up
Even when things weren't going your way
Did I ever tell you
I love you more each day?
Even if we can't be together
Because you're so far away
Did I ever tell you
I miss you everyday
Your life was taken away from you
And you didn't have a say
Did I ever tell you
What I did today?
I filled the brightest star with love
And sent it up your way

Tracy Craggs

The Highs And Lows

It's strange just sitting here
Wondering where it all went wrong
The sheer disbelief
And all the dreams - gone!

It wasn't meant to be
So many times you've heard it before
But it doesn't undo the result
And feeling sick to the core.

You had started out optimistic
That it was going to be your day
But grit and determination wasn't enough
And ____ got in the way.

At the final whistle you were shattered
And could only stand and stare
As your opponents stepped up
To collect the silverware.

The dressing room was quiet,
As you sat feeling dejected,
If you'd done this or done that,
A different score line would have reflected.

As they say, it's luck on the day,
It's either with you or it's not,
A pat on the back is some consolation,
But then again, maybe not!

But there's a new day dawning,
Get up, and dust yourself down,
You will again, have your day,
And once more, wear the crown.

Some come on, it's not all over yet,
Hold your heads up high,
Pull on the jersey one more time,
And give it another try.

Delia Finnegan

Mother

You taught these eyes to see,
and now they see without you

You taught these lungs to breathe,
and now they breathe without you

You taught this heart to beat,
and now it beats without you

You taught me to love,
and now I love you only...

Ummey Shah

Your Eyes

Your eyes look in mine
Making me lose all control
My thoughts drift away.

Charlotte Watkins

The White Chalk Sonnet

White chalk etched boldly on a red brick wall,
There in the playground for the world to see,
Our love in a heart, delicately scrawled,
Proclaiming I love her and she loves me,
One day we walked together to her door,
And gazing from beneath her long brown hair,
She said she didn't love me anymore.
The world could have stopped and I wouldn't care,
For at that moment my heart was breaking,
I was fighting back tears without success,
So young and yet my world was shaken,
By a little girl in a yellow dress.
Love stories come and most love stories go,
But this is the one I will always know.

Patricia Scurfield

Mother's Life

The worst part of a mother's life
When the chicks have grown
And flown the nest
Knowing full well we've done our best
We swell with pride, our tears we hide
Taking life in our stride.

They have to learn the ways of life
Even if it's full of strife
Some do very well to cope
We live in hope they don't take dope
We'll be there, let them know we care
Keep in touch we love you very much
If life goes well we've done well.

But how can we tell if they don't confide
Some will just hide, not knowing we're on their side
But that's the way of life when they take a wife
Have a family then they know
What mothers go through.

J Reeves

My Son

My son, I was truly blessed
The day that you were born
That first day I looked upon you
My devotion to you was sworn.

You were like a little angel
Sent down from the heavens above
When they gave you to me to hold
My heart overflowed with love.

That love, like you has grown
It's got stronger every day
And no matter what you do
It will never go away.

I want to tell you how proud I am
And lucky to be called your mother
You've gone through a tough stage of life
And beaten it as could no other.

So hold your head high my young man
Stand up proud and tall
Now that you've succeeded this era
You'll be able to succeed them all.

Catherine Haggar

What A Lovely Day

How good it is to communicate
Engage in cordial tête-à-tête
With it we share each inner thought
To embellish life with our repport.

Well of course we do it every day
And rarely do we run out of say
But with some types of casual folk
It's really best to start off with a joke.

But do remember to keep it cool
If you don't want to end up the fool
For those you'd sooner not upset
For weather yes is the safest bet.

A flippant remark to a stranger
Concerning a state of the weather
Does prove you're not an alien
Just another Homo Sapien.

Harry Derx

For My Mother

Night enfolds the home with bated breath
Death walks abroad no stranger here,
And I alone in silent thought await
The passing of a life I hold so dear.

There should be something that I need to say
But thoughts are swallowed up by my own tears,
Words of love, of comfort and regret
Lie silent and unspoken by my fears.

Memories run swiftly through my mind
Cold chapped hands from washing days,
Smells of baking, fingers in the bowl
Sunday lunchtime and the songs of praise.

Summer picnics taken in the park
Autumn gathering blackberries in the field,
Sitting in the garden shelling peas
Gathering nature's gifts for our own yields.

Christmastime when sharing in the chores
Voices joined in song like liquid gold.
Till every surface of the house was clean
And sitting quiet the Christmas story told.

Now her speech and dignity are gone
Her breathing harsh but fighting to the end.
My words come tumbling out with wretched haste
There is no time now to pretend.

Did she know that I was here at all?
In my heart I only hope and pray
That as the light went from her eyes
She heard the bird-song welcome in the day.

Lisa Fuller

You

When you're a kid you don't think about getting old,
You just enjoy life; in fact you're quite bold.
You think life will always be sweet,
You fall in love and get swept off your feet.
You find things come to an end,
You find lots of things drive you around the bend.
You have to take the good with the bad,
You just hope everything does not turn out sad.
You think people will live forever,
You find out you're not so clever.
You find out loved ones die,
You break down and cry.
You see the weeks turn to years,
You wonder if God really cares.
You think about loved ones you've lost,
You know life goes on whatever the cost.
You look at your kids, how much they have grown,
You know your life's not so bad, so don't moan.
You think about loved ones and the good times you had,
You realise you have so many memories; life's not so bad.
You hope one day you will meet again,
When God releases you from all your pain.

Thomas Tomlin

The Three Monkeys

Silent snows watch
the birds blasted,
birdsongs banished;
forests felled, earth raped.
The world, like the three monkeys,
sees not, hears not, speaks not.

Silence screams.
Death and destruction
scar the Roof of the World
where genocide rules.
The world, like the three monkeys,
sees not, hears not, speaks not.

Temple bells silenced,
monks' chants deadened.
Silence tolls, hangs in the air,
echoes the tortured and the dead.
The world, like the three monkeys,
sees not, hears not, speaks not.

The court in Hague
clamours for the Serb's head;
ethnic cleansing, his crime.
Tibet stands cleansed of Tibetans.
The world, like the three monkeys,
sees not, hears not, speaks not.

Perveez Dadachanji

For Tanya

My friend, you've gone to pastures new
With rich green grass and a glistening dew
Where you can play and run and rest
And do the things that you love best
With your loving eyes and gentle charm
You would never do anyone any harm
You were my trusting friend without compare
In my hour of need you were always there
And even though you are in pastures new
With my heart and soul I still love you.

Mark Voller

Raising A Man

I ponder the many ways to begin with raising a man,
Though not from the beginning it is.
I married who I thought was a man, no later had I said I do,
I discovered how much I really had to do.

With such little life experience of my own,
I thought oh dear, I'd rather be alone.

All but wiping he's nose,
I cook, clean and wash he's clothes.
Nobody told me I'd sold my soul,
To make a warm and loving home.

It gets better I've been told,
Hold on there girl don't be so cold.

So days go by, I nurture and feed,
The soul of the boy who swallowed me whole.
I listen and plead, I guide him and keep,
A life in which I sink deeper and deep.

My mind is a battlefield, turmoil surrounds,
The life, which I chose, was pronounced.

I gaze into your eyes, wondering,
Is this all to life, in being your wife.
What a shame, there's no one else to blame.
I close my eyes, and years go by.
You hope we never say goodbye.

Dominique Valengeon

A Guide For Life

Fill your heart with joy not sorrow,
Life on earth is all too short.
Live like there is no tomorrow.

Trust your judgment - do not follow-
Doing things you feel you ought.
Fill your heart with joy not sorrow.

Look ahead-plough your own furrow,
Never mind what others thought.
Live like there is no tomorrow.

There will be times of grief and woe,
Dwelling on them count for nought.
Fill your heart with joy not sorrow.

Be yourself and do not borrow
Others' dreams which they have wrought.
Live like there is no tomorrow.

Sit back, relax then just let go.
Savour things which can't be bought.
Fill your heart with joy not sorrow.
Live like there is no tomorrow.

Judy Sleeman

Light To Dark And Dark To Light

Do you hear the breeze whisper through the grass
As the sun sinks behind the hill
And dusk creeps from the East
The Blackbird his song sings still
The Chaffinch and the Lark are silent
Though a Wrens still in good voice
And to the dying day
The Thrush finds cause to rejoice
Then like a blanket, darkness falls
The night takes on a church like hush
And our choristers have taken refuge
In building, tree or bush
But at first light, each of our feathered choir
With a chorus to a new day, will set the land on fire.

E D Bowen

The Gates

The gates are open.
I can see him stood by them.
He's waiting for me.
Tall, gaunt, with his hounds at his feet.
His blood red eyes stare deep into my soul,
Freezing my blood.
He knows my every secret.
A bony hand signals me forward.
I can't move; terror holds me.
If I go then I am truly gone forever.
No hope; no return.
The ferryman stands patiently behind him.
Ready to take me on my journey.
My feet are lead, not moving.
I don't want to go.
I want to return.
Slowly, I shuffle towards him.
My fear growing as I pass him.
I can sense his being, his aura.
I take my place on the ferry
And become just a distant memory.

Alan Durnin

Yet, William

(RIP 15 September 2004)

He wasn't human, yet he understood me perfectly
He never talked, yet he spoke volumes
He wasn't aware, yet he knew of his existence
He couldn't reason, yet he always worked things out
He wasn't conscious, yet he was totally aware
He wasn't sentient, yet he felt pain and suffered
He was senseless, yet he intuited everything
He shed no tears, yet he often cried
He didn't laugh, yet he was so funny
He couldn't love, yet he gave so much
He was dumb, yet he was so intelligent
He had no telos, yet gave me a purpose
He had no worth, yet was valuable to me
He had no rights, yet was intrinsically good
He was just an animal, yet my faithful companion
No paradox, no metaphor, no antinomy
Just honest sentiment, I miss you,
My feline pal, William, truly.

David Hammond

I See You

I see you standing, staring
That look in your eye of urgency,
My heart in complete emergency,
With alarms ringing inside,
There's no point trying to hide,
My heart gave a shift,
For you it's a gift,
A present, not stolen and it is my pleasure,
You have it to treasure.
And in return
Something I earned, inside of me you'll forever stay,
For never another dark, unhappy day.
Poems can be cute and make you cry,
But they can never justify,
How I feel inside...

Alastair Parnell

A Passing Storm

A passing storm came rushing by
To break the summer holiday
And all the sunshine of that day
Was soon darkened by clouds
And blown away.
The story gave us a big bright
Light that shone into the night
Beautiful colours lit the
Night skies.
That made us close our
Dazzled eyes
It showed us all its light
And power, and left us
With a little shower
To water gently each flower
That gave a wink to say
Thank you for that drink
Then away went the storm
Into the night saying goodbye
Sorry to give you a fright.

Teresa Parsloe

Rest In Peace

I'm tired; I'm weary of this place
This silent stinging game
The tears, the fears, the breaking spears
The heartache and the pain

I dig my nails deep into the flame
No pain from the burn
Head hits hard on the moist floor
The world begins to turn

I'm lying here, drifting away
My heart drops like a stone
Sliced in half and left to weep
Tilted, empty, thrown

Clammy hands wrap around my arms
A new pain drives inside
Digging into those deep red grooves
I can no longer hide

I can see worried faces speak
Mouthing words that I can't hear
I turn away from the blinding light
Screaming in silent fear

My body is frozen, cold, still
My heart pumping fast
Darkness is surrounding me now
How long will this last?

Its too late now, time has passed
Allow my life to cease
End this pain, the pouring rain
Let me rest in peace

Antonia Gregory

Corporate Kiss

He sits and listens to monotoned men,
Stares at a blank wall and then
Acetate on the OHP.
Whizzing PowerPoint presentation
Of a dying corporation.
Amuses himself choosing
A biscuit you might choose,
From the selection of bland fair
In a room of bland men,
Drowning in their own mediocrity.
Weak coffee ensues, an industrial brew.
Inside he drags you around.
Has you squealing up against the flipchart.
Laughs when you try to get away
From the corner of his mind
Where he holds you, keeps you.
He wonders how long for.
Another board meeting-
Speaking of overheads,
Human resources, management courses.
Among spread sheets he spreads your legs
Climbing your thigh with his breath
While discussing micro management
With the team.
He dreams of fields, of sheets of rain,
Of the slope of your shoulder.
Misplaced in a corporate world
He clings to life among dead eyes.
Inside. Inside his heart drums to
The rhythm of your soul.

C S Rowland

In Passing

Weep not, dear heart, nor grieve me,
For our love was deep and true
Think of the love you gave to me
And the love I gave to you.

Cry not, dear heart, nor worry
For our love was both strong and deep
Think of the happiness we have had
And sleep in the deepest sleep.

Try to smile for me, dear sweetheart
Think of me holding your heart
Think of me being close to you
And nevermore being apart.

John Robert Burr

A Lesson Learned The Hard Way

If only someone had told me
many years ago
that whet you want to reap in life
is the one thing you must sow.

If only folk had told me.
'Don't hurt, or lie, or blame,
do not make others suffer,
or you will reap the same.'

If only they had told me
how hurtful words can be,
how the cruelty of the human tongue
would soon return to me.

If only someone had warned me
to love and not to hate,
I wouldn't now be hurting;
but the warning came too late.

I hurt so many people
in my younger naïve years,
and now I feel the pain they felt,
and my eyes run down with tears.

Oh, how I hurt those people,
and laughed and mocked with glee:
now all the pain I caused them
comes back to trouble me.

Such nasty things I said to them,
but what they didn't know
was, deep beneath my troubled mind,
I really loved them so

I didn't mean to hurt them,
I really didn't know
that what you want to reap in life
is what you have to sow.

Why couldn't someone tell me
the debt I must repay?
I might have listened to them,
and what they had to say.

I might have heard their warnings
and tried to change my ways.
I'm older and much wiser now
in very many ways.

I share with you this story
of pain I've had to bear,
and now I warn you, my dear friends,
and pray that you will hear.

I had no one to tell me,
but now through tears I weep:
be careful what you sow today
for tomorrow you must reap.

Geoffrey Lintott

The Pond

In a hollow in the ground,
Trees and reeds and fields surround
The pond.

Snail and frog on a log,
By the pond.

Birds sing, flap their wings,
Above the pond.

On lower note, toads croak,
On the edge of the pond.

Fish swim with tail and fin
In the depths of the pond.

Nests are made, eggs laid,
Near the pond.

Ducklings dash, make a splash,
In the pond.

Cattle wade, legs splayed,
In the muddy pond.

Winter comes, ice forms
On the pond.

Trees felled, land sells;
Fill in the pond.

Marjorie Bivins

Life At St. Whippet's

Grubby Pearson was a smelly lad, sat next to me at school
But instead of learning algebra, we always played the fool
Grandad was a ferret breeder, rosettes on every wall
Gave us both a baby one, showed us how he set out his stall
His an expert ratter, mine sits up and begs
It even hangs mums washing out, as long as you pass it the pegs
Classroom trouble started, with Grubby's furry lodger
Because it shot up his trouser leg, and bit the end of his todger
SHRIEK! He yelled and started to cry, not knowing what to do
A little like his ferret, he bit off more than he could chew
Teacher took him to matron, who couldn't believe the story
So Grubby dropped his britches, stood there in all his glory
Matron was a spinster, but she took more than a second look
Pulled of both her rubber gloves, to consult her medical book
No remedy for embarrassment, so she said to my smelly friend
Here's the school tub of Germolene, just rub a bit on the end
St Whippet's Secondary Modern saw lots of these crazy days
Everyone learning different things, in lots of different ways
There's nothing else like edumication, so my teacher said
Then pushed me in a corner, a dunce cap on my head.

Steve Coupland

The Birthday

Nobody remembered his birthday
The children had rushed off to school
His wife was late for her meeting
And somehow had seemed rather cool.

So he went to the office disgruntled
Birthdays just weren't the same anymore
His colleagues all greeted him smiling
They had never done that before.

His boss was as always charming
Attractive and younger by far
It wouldn't be being unfaithful
To go for pub lunch and a jar.

They went back to her place for coffee
He at least was enjoying his day
She slipped into something more simple
He wondered if whether to stay.

The bedroom door suddenly opened
And carrying candlelit cake in a box
Were his wife and his two smiling children
As naked he stood there in socks.

Beryl Cook

Blue Haze

Shades of blue
Shining through
Nothing stirs
Shimmers still
A silent hue
A glimmering view
As far as the eye can see.

The mist of years
Yet no tears
The bluebells lie
Lingering still
Their pleasure to unfold
Their blue so bold.

How can they know
Their awesome show
Is not long to be
Yet they simply stay
In that same way
'Til their time has come
Then we are one.

The bluebells sway
They linger still
In natures way
Their treasure to convey
Into the mind's eye
For returning to
When blue mists fly.

Valerie Nye

The Splendour And Aura Of Autumn

In England, it's the Autumn and in America 'tis the Fall
But most certainly it's the season, that really shows us all;
Such an array of blend, of rustic colours and hues
That tend to give a display, of perfect splendid views.

So many types of gorgeous flowers, and of so many a kind
But the Asters and the Dahlias, are ones that spring to mind;
For when in full bloom they are such a delight to see
And with so many different colours, Autumn is so full of glee.

At the harvest thanksgiving, we give thanks to the Lord
For the rich and ripened fruit, that we do behold,
This glorious season with its fresh harvest crops
Of apples and pears, and Kent's famous hops.

The harvest festival is such a wonderful time
As the grapes mature, so we have fine wine;
Truly the Autumn scene is just like a dream
A beautiful picture so superb and supreme
And as the leaves begin to tumble and fall
Natures seasonal story, has told it all.

Gerry Stubbs

Autumn

The year is dying
Dry leaves are flying
around in a last little dance of busyness;
their task done.
Settle down, down, down
To await your frosty crown.

A few remain though
On the stark bough
Obdurate fluttering wind-defying fingers
Whose time has not yet come
To succumb.

Why delay longer?
Are you stronger
than those which stoked and smoked yesterday's fire flames.
To make yellow light
For Autumn night.

The wind blows in vain
You remain
Your fine fewness more potently focussed and clear
Beauty bold
Decked in gold.

Stay, stay for a while
Make me smile
Beguile and bewitch with your dalliant, dangerous dance
Hold Winter at bay
For a day.

Beth Clutterbuck

He Stood Alone

He stood alone
Upon a mound
And gazed away
O'er the trees
He saw the workmen
Homeward bound
Their laughter carried
By the breeze
And as they passed
And night drew nigh
He heard the fox and
Vixen bark
And thought of the
Creatures soon to die
Prey to those hunters
Of the dark.

H Ake

Mum

Mum you are so precious
A delicate rose in bloom
You glow with love and beauty
You're the stars, the sun, the moon.

I want to tell you I love you
You're special from top to toe
You are always there beside me
And I'll always need you so.

So Mum, I give you the honour
I salute you as the best
I'd never want another Mum
You're miles above the rest.

Donna Townsend

My Grandchild

I got a funny feeling, inside this chest of mine,
when I gazed upon this little one, who looked so divine.
I heard the words your grandchild, ringing in my ears,
and somehow I was overwhelmed, and could only cry some tears.

I held you closely to me, my heart just opened wide,
It captured this special moment, and stored it safe inside.
I told you that I loved you, and a smile came upon your face,
your little hand curled round my finger, with such loving grace.

My thoughts are to protect you, from the cruel world outside,
But you're a gift from Heaven, sent to brighten up my life.
Gods plan on earth is simple, you're here to lend a hand,
Your little eyes so full of light, will help me understand.

Sadie Hearn

As The Dew Is Mankind

Oh Lord, who made the universe
And added love and laugher,
If we but trust ourselves to Thee
How can we fear here after,
And yet we may not know, or tell.
What joys Thou hast planned for us.
We only know all must be well
Since Christ has gone before us.

The caterpillar on a leaf
Would call its loss, 'bereavement';
It does not know the butterfly
Will be its life's achievement.
So we, like caterpillars, here,
Cannot predict our station,
We only know we will remain
Part of Thine own creation.

As dewdrops on a line are we,
Thy light illuminates us;
We shine, reflecting down afar,
The way Thou didst create us.
And when, at length, the line is tipped,
We slide into they Glory
To lose ourselves with Thyself…
And start another story.

Avril Lansdell

A Journey To You

Almost forever, I've been walking
In a world of glass skyscrapers
Disconnected phones
Of empty houses, dried-up hours
And broken paving stones.

A moment touched by you and I'm stopped.

In a room full of red comfy sofas
And people and parrots
And tulips and haggis
And hot chocolate fudge cake
And glittering roller skates.

And someone I might one day call home.

Louise Fazackerley

What Is Wrong With Me?

What is wrong with me?
What is wrong with being me?
The boundaries, ropes, chains in an unwanting world,
Why do they not want me as I am?
To be free from these chains, to be myself.
Is more than I can even imagine,
In a greedy world.
People, judged by looks, social status, popularity.
Nothing that matters.
Why? What did we do to become this monster?
Is God so vain that he makes us like this?
What did we do to deserve this?
There's no one there to help you when you fall, not really.
Everyone only sees themselves, no other.
When I see myself I think,
I think about all the reasons why God ruined my life.
What I did to deserve it, what I could have done to make it better,
I don't think I can anymore.
I go on waiting for something, anything.
Help me. He took my pride, my happiness, my trust.
I lost many things to that man, one thing in particular.
My mother, alone again, lost in the past. Trusting nobody.
What could I have done to stop it? Why didn't I do something?
But you can't mother, you can't.
He raped me anyway...

A M Harding

Pounding From Inside

Pounding from inside
Trying to get out
Trying to find a doorway
That will push open
Straining myself
At every possible exit
But all are shut
Fast and tight
I can see darkness
And noises whizzing
All around me
So loud
They send my mind in circles
Going no where
So I push and pound harder
Clinging to a smoldering hope
That something gives way
Then perhaps
I can escape.

Samira Nazir

16mm Black And White

If only we both could be choreographed,
our screenplay could be faultless.
Read from the auto cue,
writers would scrawl our lives, and you're the star actress.

Instead I am the extra,
who shyly stammers hi,
and knocks his way home,
normal, like a lighting guy.

I have you though,
that's the predictable happy
ending I wouldn't edit out.
And yet I know,

one day you will go out,
and leave my bedroom cold,
and our little movie
will come to a close.

As the credits roll,
our names will be there,
against a bare, black screen,
and I can't afford to see
  the reshow.

Andy Smith

Riddle

You do know my names but it doesn't matter
I'll enter your life and your world I will shatter.
I'll disrupt your senses and make you ill
I'll fray your nerves and you won't sit still.
I will make you sweat with anticipation
You'll cry and despair at your situation.
You'll curse me and thank me for what I do
Feelings of fear, helplessness and joy is what I give you.
I'll steal your breath and you'll forget how to speak
I humble the mighty and make them meek.
Within you seeds of doubt I will sow
How long this will last you will never know.
From unexpected places I can arrive without warning
The daytime, the nighttime or even the morning.
For I am what makes this world go round
It starts with a smell, a sight or even a sound.
Who am I?

Sean Anderson

Oh Elizabeth

I wish you could have been there
When the Spring burst in today
Her baskets brimming over
With a glorious array
Of blooms, plumes and fluffy down
And all that I could think of
Was wanting you around
To share
In the sublimity of her ultimate creativity
I had everything this morning - except you.

Alex Wood

The Sense Of The Senseless

I can see behind her fake smile when she looks at me.
I savour her bitterness when she speaks to me.
When we touch it is ecstasy.
We share no love because she is my enemy.

Ian Price

Moonlight

The moon looked down
On the fighting town
While enemy bombers rained death below.
The blinding flash of answering guns
Showed the city in combat with the Huns.
A smokey pall hung over all
And scorching flames licked hungrily
While endless bombs went crashing down
On gallant wounded London town.

The moon looked down on the sleeping town
And his light shone kindly overall
The ugly ruins were beautified
And the city magnificent in its pride.
The amber beams of the pale moonbeams
Drenched the city in liquid gold
The crude stark outlines softened down
And the moon felt proud of London Town.

Joan Kite

The Value Of Nothing

What a difference nothing makes!
The nought becomes the keystone
Of our sums, and in our thoughts
We're seeking that oblivion that is always out of reach.

Sometimes we need nothing.
No sound or touch or view.
Just being and not doing
Is what we long for most.

The silence and the darkness
Refresh our restless soul.
Like children to young to worry
We lie in space and time.

When words refuse to surface
Then nothing should be said.
When you know you can do nothing
To comfort or redress the sorrows of another.
Just be there an your being will do the greatest good.
Say nothing now and wait
Til it's time to live again.

Sonia Evans

Meaning

I feel,
Cheapened,
By love.
Yours or mine,
I don't know,
But it's cheap,
And it's demanding,
And it's everything sometimes.
And then, I can't stop it.
And you'd never want to.

But nor would I because,
Then it is never cheap,
It is precious,
At the time.

It becomes cheap only later,
Only afterwards,
When I'm on my own again,

And you are not.

Tracy Duckett

Portrait

The air cool and still, peaceful against the confines of the walls
The peeling paintwork revealing the layers of age
The hard wooden floor worn and grazed
The solitary sofa's velvet fabric warm and soft against my naked body
My head resting lightly on the comforting depths of the seat
The light filtering through tall windows highlighting tones of fire in my hair as it falls in dark waves
The smooth skin of my long legs wrapped around the solid frame
My lean body exposed as I lay patiently wanting
My pose graceful, strong and secure
He sits alone amongst the wooden chairs that creak with brittleness
His focus on the easel as he sketches my form with honesty
The slow strokes of his charcoal
Seem to flow across my skin with persuasion
Time melts away as he draws the shape of me with careful precision
His intense motion determined as he details
My eyes flecked with exhilaration
My passion reflected in his creative desire that he bares in his art
The sound of pencil against paper rhythmically moving
In tune with the music flooding over me
My heart seeming to beat
With a nervous vulnerability that liberates my soul
As he traces my curves I feel his hands on my taught body
The inspiration of his vision caressing my fears
His draft of me arousing a need to embrace all that I am
His interpretation of me expressing the vitality of a moment.

Jennifer Wain

The Journey Of Life

Life is but a journey, which we all travel through,
For some it is a long one, for others just a year or two,
We set off on this journey, straight from our mothers womb,
We know not when we'll reach there, but hope it isn't soon.

Whilst travelling on this journey, take a look around,
See the smiling faces of the people, who are safe and sound,
Listen to the voices, crying out in pain,
For they are the innocent victims, who will never smile again.

As you travel onwards, down life's twisting lane,
Wear a smile upon your face; it will help to keep you sane,
But if you're feeling sad and blue, reach out for my hand,
And together we will journey, throughout this tainted land.

Sometimes the sun will shine all day,
And our journeys going fine,
Then, a black cloud, will suddenly appear,
It awakens our bad memories,
And we start to shake with fear.

Sit awhile, take a rest, and let the tears flow,
Grieve with me, for those we've lost,
And talk to me of what its cost,
Even though, we both know, the pain we bear will never go.

If through our suffering, we can help another one in pain,
Then we will know our journey, hasn't been in vain.

Daphne Turner

Fools' Gold

Money is not an object of desire
Though some desire it
Money is not a work of art
Though some admire it
Money, although produced, is not a product
Though some make lots of it
Money is not a drug
Though some crave it
Money is not a cure
Though some depend upon it
Money is not like a precious gem
Though some flaunt it
Money is no friend its values are fleeting
Though some treat it as their only companion
Money is not the ultimate wisdom, nor is it wise
Though many are fooled by it.

John Hamburgh

Shades Of Autumn

Nature casts off her Summer gowns
To lay a carpet of green and gold
Dancing branches sway
As Winter's icy breath blows through
Scarecrow trees.

A leaden canopy of woollen clouds
Covers the earth with sulky tears
Moody winds moan as they sweep
Across the changing season.

Phoebe casts a shadowy light upon
A Winter darkened land
Earth shall sleep until awakened
In the morning of rebirth.

Carole Harradence

A Sun Set

As the sun sets
A burning desert runs across the sky.
While the leaves of Autumn fall.
Covering the ground with a blanket of
Multi coloured leaves.
As Autumn turns to Winter.

Pamela Javes

Onto Our Beaches

Onto our beaches
comes
the Black Death
of oily sludge.
Disaster
man-made,
could have been
avoided.
Pebbles
washed by the sea,
and dried by the sun,
lie speckled
in the tar of death.
Birds,
washed up
on the once
proud shores,
lie dead,
or clinging
to life
in oil-drenched
feathers,
and more,
much more than this
my lungs still breathe
its lingering
death…

Jade Watkins

Remember

When the clocks turn back,
And early darkness shows shop windows
Piled high with Christmas tack;
We will remember them.

When the fireworks light
The sky, and shell-like bangs and whistles
Make us jump in acted fright,
We will remember them.

In the silent land
We tried to build for heroes, factories
And pits lie still; but we will stand
And remember them:

And even though the skills
And jobs are gone, even the burger bars
Will briefly close their tills.
We will remember them,

Even as we grow old
Who were not born, we in our turn will tell
Our grandchildren what we were told,
And will remember them.

Dylan Pugh

Autumn Is The Greatest Season

Autumn is the greatest season
as the trees disown dead leaves
crunching time, debris everywhere
some lie in clusters, others scatter into hair.

Cannot wait for the Spring to lurk
exploding shades of foliage go berserk
filling colour to the bare branch and bush
only to be trampled into natures mush.

Naked branches, naked for all to see
shivering in the winds; waiting to be clothed.
Every season has its majesty
but Autumn is the greatest season
as the trees reveal their nudity.

Grant Ricketts

Villainelle

In the evenings I want to cry but cannot
A fairy dies every time you lie.

In the evenings I start to cry but I stop
Everybody wants the world to end really.

Maybe some of us don't, but the Nobodies do, the Big Ones who
wouldn't have pumped to that size if we hadn't

secretly accepted anyway, inwardly sighed
and got smaller, giving in, handing over, so they say,

a piece of ourselves, a quarter, quietly crumpling inside,
quivering, like a dying star or the red balloon in that film.
It died and was reborn as an atom bomb or something.

Weapons of Mass Destruction, 'awkward phrase',
is WOM without the B
I'm ill and in pain, scared to turn on the TV.
There's a sliver of glass in my heart slowly getting wider.

But it's just a phase, it has to be.
It's the bomb ticking away inside of me.
It's all the choked heartbreaks I didn't know I had come back to me.

Terrible fallings-out on the street at night
you hear from the window, you try to make up for
to every fairy that died, when you lied.

But the truth is always demonised, doe-eyed.
We only get to it by getting at each other
and so it only gets at us. And so it goes

world killing itself to get better, the End
is why it lives, back to the mother of all, the other, stillborn
(Never a dead faery but wants the goddam world to end)

sad dam (in bad dad) bursts in the end, it has to,
it's only sane, at the end, of all our damned denials, pain.
You like someone you call by their first name.

Either you die or get born, there it is
waters break, it's just bathwater, baby's okay
It's only the floodgates opening on the barren plain.

Andrew Shelley

Sweet Surrender

For her wish she'd live the love
That only he could bring,
And feel the joys that he had brought
When he had taught her heart to sing.

And in her wish they'd share a life
To celebrate each other,
The promise of complete devotion
with new emotions yet to be discovered.

And in his wish he'd have it all
His heart and hers were free.
But though he knew this love was real
He didn't feel that he could let it be.

So he wished for peace
And though with love he held her in his heart,
He couldn't stand the constant pain
the loss versus gain was tearing him apart.

And so it was, when she was asked
To speak of what she wanted,
And they told her that no matter what
Just one wish could be granted

Such was the love she held for him
That her words were left unspoken,
She bowed her head, granted his instead
And her wish was forsaken.

Pauline Johnston

Tree Of Life

And mother always loved trees and
Wished she knew their names and when
We walked in parks and she pushed her
Grandchild's pram she would stop and
Tell the round-eyed baby of the beauty
Of trees and how she wished she knew
Each one by name and in an old diary
She had written that the trees and the
Seas are eternal and just this morning
In the post has come a gift from the
Woodland trust of a tree chart and I
Thought on how mother always loved trees
And wished she knew their names and how
She would have loved this on her kitchen wall.

Jean-Angela Smith

Consumed By Fear

There is a nightmare trapped inside the
children that sleep,
They share a restless slumber of sorrow.
These angels wake to escape their fears,
But the heartache lingers between them.

The sinister evaluation of their innocence,
Is divided by a sharpened affliction.
The destructive sense of dutiful truth,
Causes more harm than imaginable.

The separation of sacrilegious honesty,
Is betrayed by their sensitive eyes.
And the guilt ridden tears,
Now flow as easily as the lies.

Somehow these children became adults.
They no longer wake to reconcile their fears,
But sleep to escape the nightmare of living.

Lucy-may Upton

Winter

When Winter flies her dark browed isles
O'er vernal clouds sweet daffodils
Those dew dropped miles rejoice the wood
And dawn swells bright o'er joy filled bowers
Where reigns the snowdrop pearly field
White heavenly bloused as angel's wings
O'er darling Springs brief hope filled sighs
When grey clouds flee their dark browed graves
Where azured wakes you skylarks hen
And dreams mine soul o'er rosebuds flowers
Where robin gladsome sings yet still
O'er Springtime loves sweet daffodil.

David Pirret

Precious Moments
(In dedication to my one true and undemanding love, Elkie)

The gleam of sunlight passed chinked
curtain when sleep is over and tired-ness gone,
Through open window warm scent of
roses, I arise, I stretch and yawn.

Look to the covers to see my loved
one, no expression there - still sound asleep,
I touch a lock of her red hair, a
smile appears, I kiss her cheek.

She does not stir but means to
slumber, so to recall, perchance to dream,
of our walks in woodland and
in meadow and beside fast flowing stream.

Of happy times we've spent together,
along sea front or at that fair, we
feast upon chips, fish, ice-cream,
whilst seated at a bench that's there.

In our car we seek new vistas,
mountains, lakes, life without care,
drive down country lanes then stop and
drink outside a pub somewhere.

Both night and day we're near each other,
her head would rest upon my arm,
her sweet brown eyes, they see me,
they shine her innocence, her charm.

I'd leave for work, I'd see her sadness,
was hurting to ignore,
on my return, at long days end,
she would be waiting at the door.

Just days ago the illness struck,
this unrelenting malady,
in three short weeks, no time at all,
it took my Elkie from me.

Twelve fine years we were together,
indeed was love when we first met,
her look reached out, said, ‘take me with
you, I'll be your trusting canine yet.’

For dear reader, the time that I relate,
when Elkie slept upon my bed
was only yesterday, her dreams went on
through laboured breath, her heart could
take no more, she looked at me as if to say,
‘I love you so’ of this much I am sure.

My life goes on in emptiness,
my grief I cannot hide,
I must close dear reader, for,
through tears I cannot scribe.

John Cross

How Lovely The Moon

Upon the cloudless night of jet
Long after Summer's sun has set,
She rises serene to take her place,
To reign supreme in silent grace.
She throws her beams of silvery blue,
So bathes the earth in delightful hue.
Floating, she drifts all through the night,
Shedding her glorious brightest light.
Enshrined with mist the cloak we see
Enhance much more her majesty.
Curls appear, glowing fluorescent
When she becomes the perfect crescent.
How lovely to see, on this June
The loveliest orb we call the moon.
As people past and to be
Will forever gaze with wonder at thee.

Julia Auld

Seasonal Thoughts

Spring brings the crocuses and daffodils too
All with their radiant beauty on view,
As they break through to a new birth
So thrilled to be born, they give a toast - to the earth.

Summer brings the roses in colourful array
With their pleasing fragrance, they are proud to be - on display;
In cottage gardens, tended with pride,
Where buzzing bees try to find - somewhere to hide.

Autumn brings the falling leaves
Even from the tallest of trees,
Making a carpet of russet and gold,
As they flutter to the ground to mould.

Winter brings the rain and snow,
Sometimes, rivers overflow,
The water gushing beyond control,
Then devastation - takes its toll.

Kathleen Knott

Rainy Days

Yesterday it was a rainy day
A frog, snail and slug went out to play
They hopped and squirmed about
The mud was really stout
They splashed it here and splashed it there
And then right up into the air
A butterfly passing close by
Got hit right in his eye
He fluttered down to where they were
And gave them such a nasty glare
The snail crawled off in disgust
She had had quite enough
Slug and frog carried on frolicking
Despite being given a rollicking
Soon they both became worn out
Time to call it a day hear them say
See you another rainy day
As they split up and go their separate way
Just then a Rook came diving from the sky
To have the slug he will try
The frog has other thoughts
As his body he tauts
Jumping up at the bird
I know it sounds absurd a frog attacking a bird
But his friend he will defend until the bitter end
Stretching to his full height
He gave the Rook a nasty fright
Croaking in terror it flew away
Leaving the pair to play another rainy day.

Pam Robinson

Footsteps

Footsteps on an empty shore
Golden hollows of muddy traces
A salty breeze through windswept hair
Drifting aimlessly without a care
Towering the rugged cliffs look down
And inward licks the incoming tide
To trap the frailty of man when unaware
To crush and conquer so do beware.

Gillian Gregory

The German Prisoner…

I hate this land called 'Salisbury Plain',
of cold March winds and English rain.

A soldier I was forced to be,
to fight for the 'Fatherland' you see.

I looked around, I see a barbed wire fence,
thinking to myself, it doesn't make sense.

My coat is damp, I feel so cold,
my body…I'm getting old!

They won the war, now set us free,
let me go home to my family.

I don't want to die in this desolate place-Dear God,
please answer this my prayer,
that with wife and children, my life I'll share…

David Osbourne Cox

The Fugitive

A wisp of smoke
Hangs heavily over the cubicle
The last hiding place.

Worn down by
Matrimonial nagging changing laws
Political correctness.

He seeks solitude
And one more cigarette
And then another.

Is that a noise?
A shout of triumph from the smoke police
Have they tracked him down?

Quivering yellow-stained hands
Flush the evidence, guiltily he peeps out
All clear again!

Perhaps a smoking holiday
In Thailand, country of all vices
An active smoking time.

He sidles home
Alibi dog in tow
Pepperminted up, now no one will know!

Eric Jackson

Lost Within My Dreams

Swirling mists of emptiness
Deep inside my mind
Images, a glimpse within
In the dark they hide.

Vivid thoughts and feelings
Come close then drift away
Flickering scenes, the faintest sound
The light is kept at bay.

In the depths of nowhere
Hazy memories
Secret yearnings, yet to find
Lost within my dreams.

Dawn Hadland

Beautiful Youth

Walk on by the gleaming gloaters,
Strut your stuff and flick your hair.
Feel aloof; you're being noticed-
Check your reflection if you dare.

You are the son of misled instruction;
Nurtured by mistakes gone by
To saunter to your own destruction
While whimpering women wonder why.

Some time soon you'll know the meaning
Of the portent of their praise:
Your status will not last forever.
Don't get drawn into their gaze.

So walk on by the gleaming gloaters,
Strut your stuff and flick your hair.
Feel aloof; you're being noticed-
Check your reflection if you dare.

Guy Draper

Flowers

Swing sway
Swing sway
That's what flowers love to say.

Red ones yellow ones
Green and blue
Growing in the fields
Gardens too.

Swing sway
Swing sway
That's what flowers love to say.

In the fields
Growing high
To the sky
High high high.

Swing sway
Swing sway
That's what flowers love to say.

From the ground
Growing tall
Flowers are the best of all.

Collette Lowes

Whispers

Where but in that hopeful dream
Could love find refuge still?
As shimmers on a moonlit stream
Dance to and fro at will.

The word is whisper'd with great care,
The night surrenders soon.
One heart so big that we could share
And greet this honeymoon.

Caresses touch my inmost need,
The world is left there standing,
Lust is merely love's own greed
Yet proves to be demanding.

Breeze of ages floats around
Flowing thoughts of bliss.
Music that at last has found
Perfection in your kiss.

I wish upon the brightest stars;
Tiaras in the sky ~
That Venus will seduce old Mars
And that love will not die.

Richard James

Children Of The Earth

Sunny days, playing, a parent's gentle smile
Safe and secure, at least for a while
Learning a lesson one day at a time
No cares, no worries, life should be fine

But for so many children, life's burdens are heavy
And for these burdens, small shoulders not ready
Their young hearts are pure and open to life
So why does mankind fill them with strife

Famine and war, malice and greed
These things Children Of The Earth do not need
And don't blame Mother Nature, destiny or fate
Elders, its our fault, are we too late?

To pick up the pieces and mend broken hearts
To give to all children a far better start
For they are more precious than the stars in the skies
So lets please see our love reflect within their eyes.

Anne Mcaviney

Modern Living

As I lie awake at night and contemplate my life
I feel the darkness surrounding me and draw away the light
This world is an evil place, a place without much hope
As pain and rage begins to rise
I wonder how we cope

Corporate rule is how we live, how we make our bread
We prostitute our lives to them, and nothing is ever said
Each and every one of us from birth until our death
Follow what is imposed on us
Views spoke under our breath

They say that we are civilised, that all is well and good
This utopia of genocide and streets awash with blood
Wars are fought for capital gain, we just stand and look
It seems to me that in this world
Nobody gives a f**k

When will people realise things are not as they seem
The media tells us what to think and of things we should dream
How can you say you know yourself, you are what your told
Commercial individuals
Our minds which we have sold

So as I lay awake at night contemplating this
A profound sense wells up in me that this world holds no bliss
We live, we love, we work, and die, the story of our life
The real story is but this
Our world is full of strife

Stephen Wolf

For Mum

When we were kids we didn't know
How lucky we had been
To play in rain and sun and snow
And fields of emerald green.
To build our dams across the beck
And push each other in,
To laugh and play as home we'd trek
then welcomed with a grin.
Our faces scrubbed we'd have to wait
As mother brought our tea.
We know it now but it's too late,
We were lucky you and me.

Martin Austwick